MODERN SIJO

Typeset and Printed in the United States
by EJ Company, PO Box 22612, San Francisco, California 94122

Library of Congress Catalog No. 95-068802
ISBN 0-9402049-06-3

Printed in the United States of America

ACKNOWLEDGMENT

I am deeply grateful to Ms. Margaret Richardson, president of the Daly City Creative Writers Society for her useful advice for my poems. Ms. Elizabeth St Jacques of Ontario, Canada writes Modern Sijo herself publishing a book. Special thanks for her taking time and pains for editing my manuscript with professional advice writing the Foreword of this book. Printing and book-binding were done by Mr. James Chao of E. J. Company of San Francisco whose finest work is greatly appreciated. Last and not least I am thankful to Sue, my wife who encourages me to write poems providing me much freedom and money for my works.

DEDICATION

To
Edwin A, Falkowski (1911-1989)
who inspired me to work for peace
and brotherhood of the world
with poetry

CONTENTS

Foreword I

Introduction v

POEMS:
I. MANKIND & HUMANITY 1

    1. Made colloidal 3

    2. Catchword 4

    3. Unfair 5

    4. Greed 6

    5. Unconscious 7

    6. Fishing in the mountain 8

    7. Money 9

    8. Fast bucks 10

    9.Insanity 11

    10. Crime free 12

    11. Not evident 13

    12. Conquerors 14

    13. Flies 15

    14. Euphoria 16

    15. Irresponsible 17

    16. Yackety-yak 18

    17. Mouth busy 19

    18. Silence 20

    19. In the cold 21

    20. Decadence 22

    21. Disloyal 23

    22. Raise pets 24

    23. Barking on 25

    24. Mother love 26

    25. Yin & yang 27

    26. Wicked beauty 28

    27. Values 29

    28. Phalli 30

    29. Virtues 31

    30. Loss in dignity 32

    31. True love 33

    32. Rainbow rapture 34

33. Altruism 35
34. Awaken conscience 36
35. Not envious 37
36. Hollywood 38
37. All melt 39
38. America, cut your Gordian knot 40
39. America positive 41
40. Charisma 42
41. Nixon funeral 43
42. King Alexander & Diogenes 44
43. King Wuti & monk Bodhi-Dharma 45
44. Confucius 46
45. Lao Tzu 47
46. Buddha 48
47. Jesus 49
48. Genghis Khan 50
49. Hitler 51
50. De Gaulle 52
51. Churchill 53
52. Mao & Kim 54
53. O Jackie O 55
54. Mandela 56
55. Gorbachev 57
56. Jimmy Carter 58
57. Bill Clinton 59
58. Newt Gingrich 60

POEMS:

II. NATURE & ENVIRONMENT

II. NATURE & ENVIRONMENT 61

59. On trial 63
60. Conflicts 64
61. Polluters (1) 65
62. Polluters (2) 66
33. Technology 67
64. Harmony 68
65. Offensive 69
66. Sorry souls 70
67. Bankruptcy 71
68. Die lonely 72
69. Embrace all 73
70. Sharing 74
71. The toll 75
72. Heart's torn 76
73. Paradise lost 77
74. Capricious 78
75. Winds 79
76. Gateways blocked 80
77. Peace lily 81
78. Family saga 82
79. Pyongyang my homeland 83
80. Lasting images 84
81. Changing images 85
82. Cosmic parade 86
83. Golden poppy 87
84. God's land 88
85. Spring drizzle 89
86. Spring scene 90
87. Rapture in Nature 91
88. World cheerful 92
89. Cherry blossom 93
90. Distance 94
91. Tranquil world 95
92. Thanksgiving Day 96

POEMS:

III. STRUGGLE & AGONY 97

    93. The threat 99

    94. Dharmas 100

    95. Destiny 101

    96. Cauldron white hot 102

    97. Physical prowess 103

    98. The poor 104

    99. Expand territory 105

    100. Market economy 106

    101. Deaf ears 107

    102. Myopia 108

    103. Trust 109

    104. Promises 110

    105. Words of sages 111

    106. Intangible 112

    107. Free but restrictive 113

    108. Impermanence 114

    109. Playing God 115

    110. Attachment 116

    111. Archaic & Abstruse 117

    112. Bewildered 118

    113. Hell of dearth 119

    114. Sisyphean agony 120

    115. Faith 121

    116. Fooling 122

    117. Discontent 123

    118. Karma 124

    119. Rational mind 125

    120. Vale of years 126

    121. Confession to God (1) 127

    122. Confession to God (2) 128

    123. Confession to God (3) 129

    124. Cybersyndrome (1) 130

    125. Cybersyndrome (2) 131

    126. Cybersyndrome (3) 132

POEMS:
IV. ENLIGHTENMENT & CONSCIENCE REVOLUTION ... 133

127. Universality (*Buddhatva*) 135
128. Void (*Sunyata*) 136
129. Trees 137
130. Reality 138
131. Zen monk 139
132. Humor mill 140
133. Detachment 141
134. Simple life 142
135. All happy 143
136. Enjoy alive 144
137. Echoes 145
138. Precious 146
139. Diversity 147
140. Prayer 148
141. Enlightenment 149
142. Silent afar *150*
143. Stand tall 151
144. Vignette 152
145.Eternity 153
146. Life candle 154
147. Life easy 155
148. Natural 156
149. Feel fresh 157
150. Apocalypse 158
151. Being alone 159
152. Perspiration & inspiration 160
153. Road to enlightenment 161
154. Meditation 162
155. Asceticism 163
156. Effortless 164
157. Nourish soul 165
158. Lighthouse 166
159. Possessed & obsessed 167
160. Daydreamers 168
161. Elusive 169
162. Age not 170
163. Simple & serene 171

164. My spirit 172
165. Worldly taints 173
166. Soul tainted 174
167. Soul free 175
168. Photons & souls 176
169. Intuition 177
170. No intermediary 178
171. Dizzy & eerie 179
172. Plight 180
173. Color barrier 181
174. Awakening 182

POEMS:

V. NIRVANA & SALVATION 183

175. Sense of achievement 185
176. Enjoy watching 186
177. Catch the moment 187
178. With gusto 188
179. It's today 189
180. Sojourn 190
181. Blessed 191
182. Fantasy 192
183. Mind void 193
184. Technology 194
185. Being alone 195
186. Renewal 196
187. Phantom 197
188. Discipline 198
189. Pygmies 199
190. Written painless 200
191. Nirvanic rapture 201
192. Close in view 202
193. It's Nirvana 203
194. Immortal 204
195. Resignation 205
196. Scatter quiet 206
197. Free from agony 207
198. One way street 208
199. Rest in peace 209
200. Absolute reality 210
201. Not free 211
202. Better die 212
203. Ideal death 213
204. Ode to death 214

REFERENCES 215

POEMS OF MODERN SIJO

by Kim Unsong

FOREWORD

In 1992, rules for two United States poetry contests arrived in my mailbox. Both competitions enclosed an information sheet concerning Classical Korean Sijo with two Sijo translations by Kim Unsong. That was the first I had heard of Korea's oldest and most revered poetry form and it captivated me. When my attempts earned a top prize in both competitions, I longed to learn more about the fascinating Sijo poetry form.

Kim Unsong promptly responded to my query. Since then, we have had many Sijo discussions and pleasing conversations via the mail and telephone. Among the things discussed was the need for Sijo modernization.

As with other ancient poetry forms that found their way across the ocean and time itself, it is inevitable that the Sijo too is undergoing alterations. It is important to note that alterations are not in disrespect of Korea's great poets, its people or nation. In *Modern Sijo*, Kim Unsong boldly experiments with the Sijo poetry form. Some changes are quite radical. Here, Sijo either have much longer or extremely shorter syllable counts, end rhymes, spaces between lines and titles. Lines are rather less musical than traditional Sijo. Another difference between traditional Sijo song of joy, romance, patriotism and sorrow, whereas the main focus in this five-part collection is on the moral decline of modern society, racial discrimination, disrespect for the environment among other things. Many of his Sijo are like sharp swords that slash quickly and deeply. An example (Sijo #20) :

Topless and bottomless dancing girls
generate ohs and ahs among men

What's more in store for women to expose
gushing blood or dripping semen ?

Decadent West leads the way
focusing attention on sex in critical acumen

Kim Unsong makes no apologies for the dark views found here. 'I write true to my own feelings' he says, the purpose being to stir what he calls 'a conscience revolution or spiritual renewal '. Powerfully intense, there is little question that these poems arouse deep emotions.

One is reminded of the great humanitarian and Nobel Prize winner , Albert Schweitzer, who wrote *The Decay and Restoration of Civilization and Civilization and Ethics*, which was later complied in one volume under the title *Philosophy of Civilization* (New York, 1949). Schweitzer's book begins with a pessimistic outlook which eventually turns to optimisms. Kim Unsong holds like views, his book structured in much the same way as Schweitzer.

However, Kim Unsong weaves delightful mischief through his dark world to provide small points of light. Consider for example, the following humorous Sijo with its brilliant traditional style conclusion (#6):

As election day draws near
symptoms of mysophobia flare up in the scene

Voters look for someone of great virtue
the one perfect, fair and clean

They are fishing in the mountain
seeking a saint in a world obscene

When the author refers to a much admired world figure or he speaks of his reverence for Nature, his world virtually glows. And when recalling his beloved Korean landscape and his loved ones, the depth of his tenderness unfolds as delicately as a rosebud (Sijo #80):

Mom took me to the farm half a century ago
the scents of hay still pungent

The finger-size cucumber she picked
its taste still fragrant

She now sleeps on a hill near Pyongyang
I called upon her crying but she's silent

The peace-inspiring Oriental philosophies that run through this collection are also most enjoyable. These beautifully worded Sijo present the poet's spiritual self to reflect the importance of Confucianism, Taoism, Buddhism and Zen in his life. A favorable among these is Sijo #164:

A starlet blinking faintly in the sky
a grain of sand resting on the shore

My existence in this time and space
as insignificant as a fungal spore

Yet, my spirit is as vast as the Cosmos
embracing oceans and galaxies and more

Unfortunately, moments of spiritual tranquility are fleeting and the poet's vulnerability to life's overwhelming pressures seems inevitable. He makes this startling admission (Sijo #201):

Often tempted to kill myself, yet I can't proceed

Have works to finish, books to read

Till then, I won't be freed

Aristotle, who once said *Poetry is more philosophical and of higher value than history*, and later, *dearer still is truth*, would surely applaud Kim Unsong's *Modern Sijo*. While some truths are unpleasant to face, poems here force us to look closely at ourselves and our world, and to realize the true fragility of our existence and planet. Through these pages, we are reminded that love is all encompassing. That is Kim Unsong's most powerful message of all.

Elizabeth St Jacques
Ontario, Canada
May 29, 1995

POEMS OF MODERN SIJO
by Kim Unsong

INTRODUCTION

Sijo, the classical Korean poetry, means literally "Songs of All Seasons". Its origin can be traced back to the Sylla empire (668-936) but the traditional Sijo rooted around the closing days of Koryo dynasty (918-1392) and was further developed and refined throughout the Yi dynasty (1392-1910) especially after the creation of Korean alphabet replacing Chinese characters in 1446.

Three forms of Sijo have been developed during the time; the *Chang Sijo* or long Sijo, the *Jung Sijo* or the medium long Sijo and the *Pyong Sijo* or common Sijo. The outmoded two forms are rather long and irregular and have lost their popularity. Only the common Sijo has been widely written and sung among Koreans in and out of their land (1, 2, 3, 4, 5) for over a thousand years.

The common Sijo is of a 3-line stanza each line being made up of 4 phrase groups each of which in turn consists of 3-5 syllables. As each line is made of around 15 syllables, a Sijo has a total of approximately 45 syllables. The syllable counts can be flexible especially in modern Sijo but the 3- line structure has been maintained, the first line stating a theme to hook the readers, the second twisting and expanding the theme with wit and metaphor and the last concluding or resolving the theme. During Korea's long history, tens of thousands of Sijo have been written mainly by upper class Koreans stressing their traditional values, enjoying their elegant lives and lauding beauty of nature. Still, we find many Sijo written by anonymous nobles, talented ladies and even by some commoners expressing their aspiration, passion, indignation, lamentation and resignation. A couple of examples of Classical Sijo are taken below (2).

ALLEGIANCE TO THE KING
by Chung Mongju (1337-1392)

Even if I die and die*
repeating one hundred times

Turning my bones to white lye
scattering my soul in the air

My red heart would never belie
my loyalty to the king

BLUE RAPID AND MOON
by Whang Jinnie (?-1530)

The blue rapids runs through green gorge
boast not dear how sleekly you flee*

You"ll never come back again
once you reach far into the sea

Full moon shines upon us so fresh
relax awhile, play with me

**Kim Unsong tried to apply rhymes but only to appeal to
the Western readers and they are not required in Sijo.*

Themes of Classical Sijo

In a culture of long tradition, the themes of Korean lyrics have generally been summarized in two categories; one expressing "Mot" or "elegance", the other "Hahn" or "grudge". The *a priori* Korean character is merry and sunny venting an air of elegance in their ethos yet after centuries of foreign invasion and domestic exploitation a lingering pathos clouded his character resulting in an abiding grudge. Reflecting these rather conflicting sentiments, classical Sijo were written to express their feelings largely along their traditional esprit.

I examined some 300 sijo in an anthology of over 5000 classical Sijo poems (5) and classified them by traditional themes. The results are rather striking as we see in Table l.

TABLE 1. Frequency of themes of 300 Classical Sijo sampled from over 5000

I. Elegance series (Mot) .... 61.0 %
    1. Rhapsodic jubilation .... 31.5 %
    2. Patriotic dedication 17.7
    3. Romantic flirtation 11.8
II. Grudge series (Hahn) .... 39.0 %
    4. Lamenting indignation .... 20.4 %
    5. Passive resignation 18.6

Format of Classical Sijo

The 3 line format of Sijo is not unlike the deductive logic of Syllogism; the first and second lines serving the major and minor premises and the last line the conclusion. Yet Sijo is no Syllogism executing a deductive reasoning; it is a lyric form brewed naturally in the long tradition of Korean poema constantly bubbling in their hearts. Its imagery fresh, its passion intense, its metaphor profound and its message sincere while the Chinese Chuehchu or truncated verses would take pains relishing cumbersome tonal patterns of words and foot rhymes to enhance a musical effect, while the brief Japanese Haiku calls for polished images leaving no room for the Muse to dance about.

Modern Sijo

Departing from the Classical poems, modern Sijo have taken a road of revolution since early fifties of the 20th century. Their subjects, themes and techniques no longer follow the aristocratic elegance and the commoners' abiding grudge. In the light of democracy, modern Sijo are wide open, their subjects and themes diverse, their imagery fresher, their expression delicate, their metaphors subtle, their passion dynamic often decadent boldly blending modernist trend of western poetry. In a sense, modern Sijo largely have turned more sophisticated than before. Contemporary Sijo writers generally ignore the yoke of syllable limit only keeping the format of 3-line stanza.

After the publication of my booklet *100 Classical Korean Poems (Sijo)* in POET, an international Monthly in 1986 (1) and books (2, 3), Sijo are becoming popular with Western poets. In the past several years I have served the judgeship in annual Sijo contests held in California and Arizona. Some Western poets are quite prominent now. For example Elizabeth St Jacques of Canada has repeatedly won top prizes in Sijo contest. Her Sijo collection *Around the Tree of Light* (6) is to be published in 1995.

The purpose of my Sijo book

I am eager to express my grave concern on the widespread depravity of humanity and the seemingly hopeless degradation of global environment. The homocentric concept lauded in the Bible is steadily out of fashion. The salvation of humanity and protection of environment can only be achieved by a conscience revolution or spiritual renewal. The universe including the earth is for all things to exist. The traditional human centered world view has become no longer valid in light of the great predicament generated by modern civilization. Mankind can only survive existing in harmony with Nature. It is the Universalism (Buddhatva) propounded earlier by Buddha. A mosquito, stone, tree, river, mountain, sun and moon, stars and galaxies all have equal right to exist or *raison d'être* as well as mankind. Exploiting fellow humans and Nature in the name of progress, modern science and technology have done great disservice to Buddha's teaching. The Universalism shall be the guide for a conscience revolution of the world. A modern Sijo format seems to serve a convenient vehicle for that purpose.

Every attempt was made to innovate the themes, subjects and techniques used in the Classical Sijo to adapt for modern times. The leisurely tempo, gentle pace and generic outlook of the world and Nature taken by the ancient Koreans are no longer acceptable in the modern world where humans are constantly pressed by squeezing space and time. While retaining the 3-line stanza format, I carefully weighed out words to relish fresh imagery, meaning and metaphor necessary to appeal the taste of modern folks. Using alliterations and extensive rhyming I intended to please my Muse as well as the readers. Some emotion packed words may strike harsh chords yet many open-minded hearts will be soothed.

My poems may offend some readers but I make no apologies for being true to my own feelings.

My book may be the first attempt to modernize Sijo widely in a world scale. In view of the globalization of the politics, economy and culture of this century, this book is a cultural adventure. I cannot be certain that the modern Sijo I am presenting here would be accepted or rejected. I only hope my book would be controversial enough to provide an opportunity for the advancement of our great poetry, the Sijo.

Organization of the book

Under the influence of modernism, my Sijo of over 200 have been divided into several themes focusing attention on some contemporary cultural and environmental crises; (1) Mankind and Humanity (2) Nature and Environment (3) Struggle and Agony (4) Enlightenment and Conscience Revolution (5) Nirvana and Salvation. On each theme I expressed my serious and sincere concern of the civilization on trial and the humanity in crisis. Poems range from pessimistic to optimistic starting with gloomy pathos ending with blooming ethos. It is my firm view the salvation of civilization, the renewal of humanity and the restoration of environment can only be achieved by a conscience revolution or a renewal of human spirit. Traditional religions and the much ballyhooed market economy backed by modern technology have largely failed in their mission. In sections 4 and 5 some recipes for enlightenment are presented.

POEMS

I. MANKIND AND HUMANITY

The millennium effort of religious teachings and moral guidance and centuries of technological development have failed so far to correct the moral depravity which has gone on a steady downtrend. Fratricide among different ethnic and ideological groups has been intensified even after the post Cold War era. Traditional religions have failed to curb human avarice and technological advances keep fanning the trend of consumption of limited global resources, polluting natural environment with waste products. Politicos are simply impotent in a world where morality is tarnished and authority is downtrodden and unruly mobs turn decadent running wild to destroy existing law and order. Some notable historical characters are sung in my Sijo.

1. MADE COLLOIDAL

Man stands tall above all beings

never can reach God's holy precinct

Often playing God

his reasons transcend the bestial instinct

Yet his cells are made colloidal

so his being only indistinct

2. CATCHWORD

No man is created equal

in skills and intelligence

Democracy ignores the fact

being only instrumental for political convenience

I'm weary of the catchword

with cynical indifference

3. UNFAIR

World population mushrooms
civil unrest brews everywhere

People struggle for existence
tempers flare

Rain and shine the weather uneven
rich and poor life is unfair

4. GREED

Roosting, a bird takes

only a single branch that would accede

Thirsty, it drinks

only a few drops of water it may need

Man would take the whole tree

and the entire river through greed

5. UNCONSCIOUS

Driven by animal instincts
many people are in great need

Warm hearts and cold brains seldom functional
life goes on by blind greed

Conscious minds are asleep
seem dead indeed

6. FISHING IN THE MOUNTAIN

As election day draws near
symptoms of mysophobia flare up in the scene

Voters look for someone of great virtue
the one perfect, fair and clean

They are fishing in the mountain
seeking a saint in a world obscene

7. MONEY

God, king, father are pinnacles of authority

Fast being abdicated losing dignity

In the modern world money is the deity

8. FAST BUCKS

Sensationalism leads the way
tapping wacky events is the priority

News' main concern
seems to arouse public curiosity

Make the bucks fast
who cares for morality

9. INSANITY

Sitcoms, talk shows simply nauseous

eliciting instant guffaws alluding obscenity

Mixing crude witticism

their arts lack ingenuity

In a world so frivolous

they are out to sell insanity

10. CRIME FREE

Ignoring clutches of moral codes

many youth do anything they like being free

Alcoholics, drug addicts, gunslingers

having heyday in street jubilee

Laughing at crime-free countries

being underdeveloped or dirty

11. NOT EVIDENT

In the world of post Cold War

ethnic wars violent

Under the guise of humanism

fratricide ever rampant

In the animal world

it is never evident

12. CONQUERORS

The yellow hordes with bows and arrows

stampeded Europeans in awe

A-bomb blasts blossomed mushrooms in skies

Americans went hee-haw

Crooner Jackson conquers the podium in peace

world cheers, the blacks caw

13. FLIES

Peddlers, politicians, partisans

spread lies

Selling their goods

in bloodshot eyes

The world would be serener

without flies

14. EUPHORIA

In the land of freedom and modernism

troupes of avant-garde go in great stride

Morale high, demeanor rude, tempers hot

narcissists, pygmalions all march side by side

Old values trashed, authorities downtrodden

their utopian euphoria ride the tide

15. IRRESPONSIBLE

Media people just talk talk

cacophony echoes through the air

Seldom prudent

they puff and piffle everywhere

Words irresponsible

little to share

16. YACKETY-YAK

Truth transcends words
that can never exhaust it

Impulsive talkers are potential liars
lacking true wit

Taoist and Zen monks talk little
drunkards and punks yackety-yak, never quit

17. MOUTH BUSY

Eyes, ears and nostrils

see, hear and smell in pair

Eating, drinking, talking

a single mouth takes care

Let it work prudent little

not to exceed its share

18. SILENCE

Impulsive talkers

cover their weaknesses untold

No matter how passionate they talk

their stories can hardly be sold

Silence often overcomes the speech

turning it to gold

19. IN THE COLD

The Greek never meant the Olympic events
to promote superegos craving gold

Enjoy sex in private and sport in public
so we are told

Breaking rival Nancy's leg
Tonya drives the fans away in the cold

20. DECADENCE

Topless and bottomless dancing girls

generate ohs and ahs among men

What's more in store for women to expose

gushing blood or dripping semen ?

Decadent West leads the way

focusing attention on sex in critical acumen

21. DISLOYAL

Orchards bear fruits
domestic animals are loyal

They are devoted to their hosts
little known of their betrayal

Trouble with human world
many disloyal

22. RAISE PETS

Pets are more loyal than children
demanding little else over their basic necessity

Few parents joyful over their kids
many being disappointed from their activity

The entire globe is being crowded
we'd rather raise pets than children of infidelity

23. BARKING ON

Podge, a dog resembling a panda
runs patches of black and white in her system

When the quake hit Kobe, her owner buried deep
lain unconscious in the mayhem

She kept barking loudly for 53 hours
until rescuers came to save them

24. MOTHER LOVE

A dog abandoned in remote Island
bears 5 puppies cute brown

She swims across the strait over a mile
to feed self full in a town

She returns to breast-feed her litters
swimming the sea head up tail down

25. YIN AND YANG

Protons attract electrons forming an atom
while the same particles repel the other

Same laws of magnetism work for human
yet homosexuals embrace one another

Ignoring the Cosmic rule of Yin and Yang
they seem never to bother

26. WICKED BEAUTY

Deliberately enticing men

to be palsywalsy

Only to accuse the namby-pamby

unilaterally faulty

Beware of women

of wicked beauty

27. VALUES

Given a bone the dog wags its tail

appreciating the donor from its heart

A free lunch pleases many

while for more money the rich ever smart

Meeting own ends

senses of value far apart

28. PHALLI

"Guns are a phallic symbol" said Freud,
"but my cigar is a cigar", sounds unfair

In America gun slingers run amok
any time anywhere

O the phalli, real or symbol
just nuisance if abused, beware !

29. VIRTUES

Having sex

we often lose freedom instantly

Talking nonsense

we lose dignity inadvertently

Virtues hard to maintain

unless we check actions constantly

30. LOSS IN DIGNITY

A sex act brings partners immediate equal

after a blind brief ecstasy

Transcending gaps of intelligence

falling deep in fantasy

The superior one is now bitterly remorseful

over a colossal loss in dignity

31. TRUE LOVE

A burning desire for sex is no love
it's only a thirst

With a sexual rendezvous
amorous blood boils and bubbles burst

Only when emotions simmer down
will we in the true love be immersed

32. RAINBOW RAPTURE

Vanity and greed blind us
making life miserable in daily strife

Staying alive is God-blessed
anything beyond is a bonus for life

What rainbow rapture a couple get
leading the day as husband and wife

33. ALTRUISM

Soft and clean in white, yellow, pink or blue
Kleenex waits for us in neat array

Removing dirt of others
it's soiled, worn and torn

It works quietly never nagging nor bragging
a supreme symbol of altruism

34. AWAKEN CONSCIENCE

Crimes will not be stopped

only by force

Increasing police, building more jails

are not a good recourse

Educate youth

awakening their conscience to remorse

35. NOT ENVIOUS

In arenas of cultural gatherings

Americans run amok triumphant

Belittling other peoples

as a bunch of abject sycophant

Behold the snails crawling

never envious of the stampeding elephant

36. HOLLYWOOD

Sexploitation titillating

romances elegant

Western movies thrilling

actions violent

In a drowsy world American cinemas refreshing

scenes extravagant

37. ALL MELT

Colors beautiful

discrimination improper

Racial harmony brings

the world to prosper

All melt in America

accommodating all superduper

38, AMERICA, CUT YOUR GORDIAN KNOT

Free the drug trades

its war will instantly cease

Ban the hand guns

crimes will rapidly decrease

Enforce the universal vote

elections will run serene in peace

39. AMERICA POSITIVE

Dresses informal, salads edible
water potable

Highways free, wide, straight
work, idle, play all probable

People colorful, talents vary
youth wild yet affable

40. CHARISMA

With charisma, the oratory is of little value

a silent smile can be attractive

Even the rich and famous

their power often goes inactive

It's a God-given charm

intangible yet highly active

41. NIXON FUNERAL

Burying in the ground

many die helpless and nameless

A funeral is being held now

ceremonial splendor peerless

Heroes bury their bones

but their names unburied, remain timeless

42. KING ALEXANDER AND DIOGENES

"What can I do for you Diogenes ?"

"no thanks, I'm all right"

"You're not worth of my favor

only worth of me doing all under my might"

"Just say so I can show you my generosity"

"just stay out of my sunlight"

43. KING WUTI & MONK BODHI-DHARMA

"Temples built, scriptures printed, monks trained,

as a king am I worth anything ?"; "nothing !"

"What's Buddhism ?"

"wide and void and no blabbing"

"Who's the man facing me?"

"don't know !"; disgusted the monk left the king

44. CONFUCIUS

Feudal lords fighting futile wars

your teachings were largely refused

They were blinded by greed and vanity

their powers had long been abused

25 centuries after you left

people are still confused

45. LAO TZU

Disgusted he kicked his desk away

leaving the court so rotten

When he knocked the gate of Han Ku Pass

guards opened it to the philosopher they cotton

The heavenly net never coarse

the fugitive was caught and his Taoism not forgotten

46. BUDDHA

The Capella palace of prince Siddhartha

no place for glory

Young princess and baby

no objects for jubilee

Until enlightenment struck him

after a 6 year meditation under the linden tree

47. JESUS

Born humble to rise heavenly glory

dedicating his only life redeeming all sin

In a bubbling world down on earth

fratricide continues, none ever win

Only by repenting and loving enemies

will the paradise open up for us all in

48. GENGHIS KHAN

To save own skins or get promoted

sycophants lick boots of dictators

Expressing excessive loyalty they appear so humble

before the cold eyes of interrogators

Genghis often chopped heads off the traitors

betraying own chiefs before the spectators

49. HITLER

Dreaming of an evil empire

through racial and ethnic purity

Perished are millions of Jews and gentiles

scorched are continents under fire of atrocity

A devil spooked behind a human mask

shall never be forgiven in the name of humanity

50. DE GAULLE

The seven footer with a prominent nose
his mind being occupied by French glory

Fighting Nazis scuttling NATO
his Olympian eyes overview history

Ever dreaming of a lasting peace on earth
establishing the great USE* in the territory

*United States of Europe

51. CHURCHILL

Warrior, writer, painter, statesman
a multiple genius peerless in history

Cracking Nazi strongholds, tearing down the iron curtains
he helped bring freedom to victory

In the totalitarian wasteland
he planted seeds of democracy

52. MAO & KIM

Mao Tze Tung and Kim Il Sung

the prominent chairmen of China and Korea

People may jeer and cheer

in own mythopoeic fantasia

Following Ghenghis Khan

they were the superstars played in Asia

53. O JACKIE O

Straight under pressure

O Jackie O, how gracious

Smiling under tragedy

O Jackie O, how courageous

Majestic under pandemonium

O Jackie O, how gorgeous

54. MANDELA

For racial and national freedom

you fought fearful odds winning a victory

Out from the jail of a quarter Century

you now sit on a throne so lofty

Black hero Nelson Mandela

The rising star to heavenly glory

55. GORBACHEV

Even successful

revolutions often go gory with insanity

Downing an evil empire of the century

you made it bloodless restoring humanity

Gorbachev, the hero of heroes

your courage and intelligence will shine for eternity

56. JIMMY CARTER

Ever hopeful never restful

you're a lightning rod of humanity

Prying open iron-gates, soothing frozen hearts

you bring on earth peace and sanity

You're no man of charisma

only a humble servant of divinity

57. BILL CLINTON

Whores, news-hounds, hypocrites, partisans

stop now; it's enough

Stop rocking the boat Clinton's steering

the ocean is rough

Leave him alone, let him be president

he's smart, his job is tough

58. NEWT GINGRICH

Bright-eyed brilliant House Speaker
a God-blessed man of vision

For 40 years under the shadow of FDR
Democrats hedge in indecision

American evolution shall proceed
in the era of hitech and television

POEMS

II. NATURE AND ENVIRONMENT

With the advance of technology, the environment of air, water and soil has been grossly abused accumulating industrial wastes polluting the globe, breaking food chains, even exterminating thousands of precious living species. Mother Nature has now turned to retaliate mankind. Production and consumption beyond the human need are in fashion in advanced industrial countries and the less advanced countries are all out to mimic advanced ways of living. Without conservation and recycling of the limited natural resources of earth, the environmental degradation can only be aggravated leading to a demise of mankind.

59. ON TRIAL

Crowds intolerable, noise unbearable

air and water filthy, toxins soaking the earth

Nowhere and none are safe

depriving our mirth

Civilization is now on trial

whether mankind will make life worth

60. CONFLICTS

Compressing time and space

technical bumper crops increase

Chasing gods away

wars continue in the name of peace

As civilization sweeps the globe

conflicts never cease

61. POLLUTERS (1)

Some 4 % Americans consume 40 % global resources
depleting the wealth of the earth

Fanning consumption in every nook of the world
the globe becomes polluted

Nature continues to devolve
men are out to create values of little worth

62. POLLUTERS (2)

In the name of freedom Americans talk loud
often behaving rude breaking propriety

In the name of progress they waste resources
pollute environment boasting technological superiority

The people of the 3rd world feel queasy
living in great anxiety

63. TECHNOLOGY

Technology brought comfort and convenience

with much money

Distribution of the wealth is never even

throwing the world into a whirlpool of acrimony

Industrial revolutions proceed

breaking harmony

64. HARMONY

Children are naive with Nature

perceiving her in their rapturous intuition

Grownups court her for own benefit

pursuing their material goals into fruition

Youth live in harmony with her

while adults stand in opposition

65. OFFENSIVE

Fanning greed

global capitalism gets intensive

Puncturing holes in the heavens

pollution extensive

Lord never meant to create man

so offensive

66. SORRY SOULS

Many rich and famous

reluctant to share

Old virtues drying up

like the mist in the air

Mother Nature hears the sorry souls

lamenting everywhere

67. BANKRUPTCY

Over and around San Francisco Bay
cars crawl, ships swarm, planes roar

Natural serenity and beauty have long faded
cacophony rises and wastes pile up galore

After a bankruptcy of Mother Nature
the homocentric earth can sustain no more

68. DIE LONELY

Man kills tigers, rhinos, elephants

for skins, horns, ivory

Cleaning up rain forests

for farms and shelters he is busy

After Mother Nature goes into bankruptcy

one day man will die lonely

69. EMBRACE ALL

Because of racial and cultural differences

people discriminate each other

Prejudice will remain

one way or another

Mother Nature embraces all

spicy varieties thrive together

70. SHARING

Mother Nature shares with us everything she has

yet, we're seldom willing to do so

Not only are we stingy with materials

but with smiles, words and hearts also

Sharing with others brings pleasure

returning us many fold over they owe

71. THE TOLL

On January 17, 1994

erupted is a 30 second quake

Mother Nature goes berserk

people die, structures break

Over a billion dollars second

the toll people to take

72. HEART'S TORN

In the LA quake many die, go homeless
People scurry about

In a tent village
a baby just born

In mom's arms it's asleep
her heart's torn

73. PARADISE LOST

The Universe was meant to be a paradise
all creatures come to interfuse

Deliberately destroying the Nature
human tyranny continues

Under a homocentrism the paradise lost
"Eden on Earth" only a utopian news

74. CAPRICIOUS

Quakes, tornadoes, floods, droughts
Mother Nature vents her fume

Then she smiles again in the sun
skies blue, fields green, flowers bloom

Capricious, she tears off her silken fabrics in a fit
only to weave back again on her loom

75. WINDS

Winds blow, their action effortless

Breezy or stormy, their power limitless

Work as they please, their freedom boundless

76. GATEWAYS BLOCKED

Congestion, confusion continue

everywhere metropolitans deadlocked

Exodus in weekends

turns streets and freeways grid-locked

Roads to paradise are a long way off

gateways to Eden blocked

77. PEACE LILY

Lush green leaves sway

pensive in breeze

Bright white flowers shoot up

exalting on long peduncles at ease

With pride and elegance

it greets me to please

78. FAMILY SAGA

On a barren hillside, a clone of golden poppy
grew with a family of seven

Fighting a six-year drought
they struggled along under the glowing sun

Thanks to plenty of rain this year
they turn vigorous now blooming into eleven

79. PYONGYANG MY HOMELAND

Spring breeze brings soft drizzle
frost-bitten flower branches sway serene

The Moran Hills overwhelm with romance
painting azaleas pink on a canvas light green

Overlooking the jade Daedong River
a halcyon day languishes over the scene

80. LASTING IMAGES

Mom took me to the farm half a century ago

the scents of hay still pungent

The finger-size cucumber she picked

its taste still fragrant

She now sleeps on a hill near Pyongyang

I called upon her crying but she's silent

81. CHANGING IMAGES

Snow-capped mounts soar into the blue sky

head-down upright, I see a holy island in the lake

Images set firm

mistaken views to take

Metaphors boundless and images infinite

demanding constant change in our wake

82. COSMIC PARADE

Stars blink in skies serene
fireflies flit over the field of hay

In the night lamps blossom in the dale
in the lake daffodils dance the day

Cosmic parade displays all the year round
life goes on splendid all the way

83. GOLDEN POPPY

In foggy chilly morns
you roll up your golden crown tight

Come high noon sunny and balmy
you yawn opening the crown full yellow bright

In afternoons wide awake under blue skies
you dance under cascades of sunlight

84. GOD'S LAND

A good earth sans flowers
would be skies without the sun

Mother Nature keeps caressing souls
making lives great fun

Flowers bloom the year round
California, a God's land second to none

85. SPRING DRIZZLE

Hills green, streams gurgle, sea gulls flap

foghorns yawn near the Angel Island

Hopes awakening in whispering rains

aromas seep deep from pine glands

Spring drizzle over the Bay Area

brings joy for all in the arid land

86. SPRING SCENE

Walking over the mountain pass
along the breezy shore of crystal lake

Pasticci of spring festival
open my ears and eyes wide awake

Sights, sounds, scents fresh
what a lucky break

87. RAPTURE IN NATURE*

Stretching over 10 thousand Li

blue heavens loom

Clouds hover, rains scatter

skies gloom

Mounts quiet, none present

streams murmur, flowers bloom

*adapted from the poem by Whangshan Ku

88. WORLD CHEERFUL

Bees buzz, cocks crow, crickets chirrup

natural symphony plays earful

Expressing emotions our words often harsh

actions fearful

Only when we learn from Nature

can the world be cheerful

89. CHERRY BLOSSOM

With pride and honor cherry flowers
blossom bright, fragrant and tender

In unison
they challenge and surrender

Responding to the whispers of spring breeze
they bloom and doom in splendor

90. DISTANCE

Blinking stars in the ebony night
we're thrilled with hopes they inspire

Soaring mounts over the clouds
their mystic beauty we admire

Being detached and distanced
values run ever higher

91. TRANQUIL WORLD

The world of flora and fauna
rich in variety

Living serene sans fratricide
flood and fire the only anxiety

Dismissing the technological ting-a-ling
their world far more tranquil than our society

92. THANKSGIVING DAY

America is blessed with corn and beans

in the bumper year

Signs of peace and prosperity

abundantly clear

I thank God for being alive

anything beyond is a bonus quite dear

POEMS

III. STRUGGLE AND AGONY

Survival of the working folks can only be met with struggle under agony. Agonies of the underclass mount daily leading them into jobless, hopeless and homeless. Life is God-blessed and each shall live the day with gusto. Downgrading life is a great sin. It is imperative to lead a creative and positive life. Far from resolving problems arising from the struggle of life, traditional religions have failed to allay agonies of people. Much ballyhooing modern technological advances often aggravate their predicament by the deliberate art of dehumanization.

93. THE THREAT

Buddha talks mercy

or Karma would aggravate perpetrators

Christ preaches love

or hell for the violators

Mohammed commands holy words

or a holy sword shall befall the traitors

94. DHARMAS

Buddha's lighthouse keeps burning

in the sea of agony, wrecked ships stall

Sailors argue how to rescue passengers

many panic in a close call

In the Dharmas of Tripitaka

only words flood drowning all

95. DESTINY

Among zillions of heavenly bodies

only the earth blessed with the sun in its proximity

No matter how exalting or depressing

all doomed to die in finity

In the meantime life goes on

forgetting destiny

96. CAULDRON WHITE HOT

Gunshots cracking

people alert

Washing blood stain with blood

ethnic cleansings done with ethnic dirt

The globe is like a cauldron white hot

steaming molecules flying pert

97. PHYSICAL PROWESS

Applying physical torture
to free mental stress

Early Buddhists begged foods, wore rags
often ate animal droppings during illness

Modern folks never bother
keeping their corporeal prowess

98. THE POOR

Faces drawn and dull after their daily works
seeing no smiling sun in the heavenly place

Feel dizzy and drowsy, moody and morose
many express little of human grace

Driven by cogwheels of the industrial world
enslaved in tight frames of time and space

99. EXPAND TERRITORY

Gurus and politicians are skilled salesmen
eager to sell goods in smoke screens of oratory

Gospels full of rhetoric
political pledges hunky-dory

All out to fulfill egos
dead set to expand own territory

100. MARKET ECONOMY

Even ugly faces are marketable
the contest rough

Interviewers reject most of them
because they are not ugly enough

In market economy
competition is real tough

101. DEAF EARS

Sages exhaust words
priests only rehash them to deliver

In modern days people struggle for life
seeking new values their minds quiver

Turning deaf ears to holy talks
old teachings often go fizzle and flivver

102. MYOPIA

In every nook and corner of the land
gunslingers spray bullets often with impunity

Lacking are the fundamental solutions
educating youth of values and dignity

Increasing police and building more prisons
myopic politicians play games, what a pity !

103. TRUST

The world turbulent and violent

morality rotten to the core

People suffer from constant misgivings

like churning waves by the shore

Politicians are out to help

many don't trust them anymore

104. PROMISES

Religions promise paradise

where milk and honey flow

Science and technology propound progress

in dazzling glow

Yet, misery is only aggravating

promises broken, hopes low

105. WORDS OF SAGES

Confucius, Buddha, Christ, Mohammed
all talk wise and so right

Technological advancement
forces modern men to run and fight

Hard to implement their teachings
in a world galloping day and night

106. INTANGIBLE

In wars, quakes, fires and floods

every day thousands die

Because of hunger and diseases

agony and misery multiply

God's hand intangible

in vain people cry

107. FREE BUT RESTRICTIVE

Drugs and gods

addictive

Without their constant supply

mortals largely get inactive

Being free from them

I live rather restrictive

108. IMPERMANENCE

With pomp, power, pledges
prominent heroes appear

Once they are down
enemies cheer, admirers tear

Impermanence is Cosmic Law
in vain, mortals cheer and jeer

109. PLAYING GOD

Bible says God created man in His image
to manage everything on earth

If He is the supreme being of goodness
so would be His copy equal worth

Playing God, many world leaders abuse power
creating God in his image at his birth

110. ATTACHMENT

Snails crawl across the freeway
daisies bloom in cracks of pavement

Risking their very life
in existential sentiment

Darwinian struggle, Schpenhaurian Wille
or Buddha's blind attachment?

111. ARCHAIC & ABSTRUSE

Bible is deliberately written in archaic words

modern poets love to use words abstruse

Hiding under veils of mystery

they hope to attract the bemused in their caboose

Archaic and abstruse words

will only bring the confused to vamoose

112. BEWILDERED

Sadam seeks Allah for favor

George prays to Jesus for a victory

Gamblers implore Lord for gains

killers beg for mercy

Bewildered God knows not what to do

better punch their noses granting no glory

113. HELL OF DEARTH

Jehovah blessed man
to have domain over all things on earth

Buddha decreed universal mercy and equality
announcing every life is worth

Modern industry is out to change the status quo
bringing us all in a hell of dearth

114. SISYPHEAN AGONY

Three clones of black nightshade grow vigorous
on a fertile patch of soil in the wayside

Rabbits pluck away all leaves
leaving a few pale blue flowers sad-eyed

They regenerate foliages in a few weeks
only to be eaten away by the predators wild-eyed

115. FAITH

Rooted deep in the earth

plants are immobile very vulnerable indeed

In their saga, the odds overwhelm

winds whack, rains rattle, animals stampede

An unflinching faith toward the sun and soil

transcending the ordeals, their life shall proceed

116. FOOLING

Hypocrisy rampant in religious jungles

using shibboleths like "love" or "mercy"

Many of them are hostile among themselves

after their sectarian interest and money

How can they face God

fooling friends and family ?

117. DISCONTENT

Pink pimpanels cute small, eucalyptus elegant tall

Creeps crawl the ground, eagles cleave the air

Content with what they are and have

all things keep their turfs then and there

Humans are discontent over own lot

eager to change status feeling unfair

118. KARMA

Buddha's causality law states

from good must come good, from evil the evil

In modern days moral abuse rampant

people concern little to be civil

Until all reach Nirvana

Karma will continue paying the devil

119. RATIONAL MIND

People busy eyes blind
industrial tyranny leads the way

Brains scattered by overwhelming information
many no longer aware of the smiling sun of day

Ever nervous, passions rise, tempers flare
rational minds hard to come to play

120. VALE OF YEARS

Alternating agony and ecstasy
my life path strewn with joy and woe

Bidding farewell to enter my Shangri-La
seems near but when I don't know

Beating many sages and heroes in all ages
my vale of years still on the go

121. CONFESSION TO GOD (1)

Creating all shades of humans and things
you sure love spicy varieties

Racial conflicts continue
killing and maiming in many societies

Why create Satan and do nothing
for culprits doing such atrocities

122. CONFESSION TO GOD (2)

Being omniscient, omnipotent, omnipresent

your moral straight jacket never let's go free

Your holy words impressive

yet the surrealistic jargons bewilder me

Many clergymen who play God

are proven phony to be

123. CONFESSION TO GOD (3)

Your tolerance great

even allowing evils to pass by

Giving equal time and opportunities

for all come to try

You are absolutely fair

sentencing all to die

124. CYBERSYNDROME (1)

Cybertribes having heyday
running rapid on the information superhighway

Memory chips shrinking to molecular size
while their capacity expanding to terabytes

In calculating speed and memory capacity
the cybernetic oxymoron excels neurons in a way

125. CYBERSYNDROME (2)

Through networks of internet
cyberbusinesses bloom into Americana

Cyberdata ticking along cacophonous
everyone shouts but none listen

Losing human touch
cyberspace is no nirvana

126. CYBERSYNDROME (3)

Completely dehumanized

cyberspace surreal

Cyberbooks written without an editor

cybersex performed without a partner

Humanism calls for no hitech

nostalgic after lo or no tech that's real

POEMS

IV. ENLIGHTENMENT AND CONSCIENCE REVOLUTION

At the end of 20th century our civilization is on trial and humanity in crisis. We can survive only through enlightenment and conscience revolution not by the practice of traditional religions nor by the advancement of modern technology but by all being Cosmic conscious. Blind drive motivated by greed, vanity or curiosity can only be checked by philosophical awareness and universal mandate implementing the Cosmic Laws of Impermanence and the finite destiny of all things.

127. UNIVERSALITY *(BUDDHATVA)*

Declaring Universality in the world

Buddha exalts ignoring idiosyncrasy

All things endowed with finite life

existing under equal opportunity

Modern men are far away

from heeding his Decree

128. VOID (*SUNYATA*)

The Cosmos is blank

no beginning, ending or substance

Anyone seeking a tangible truth

will be disillusioned widening the distance

Life insubstantial

because of the void in existence

129. TREES

Cornered, animals squeak, squeal, scream
people sick, panic, kick

Badly battered and even cut to bleed
trees stay calm never to panic

Revealing Cosmic virtue
trees stand serene and chic

130. REALITY

Science serves better

than blind faith in despondence

Yet it tells us

only a part of our experience

Reality is the closest

to our existence

131. ZEN MONK

He needs no mirror to view his image
has no calendar to tell the date

No house to keep, no book to read
no TV to watch, no woman to mate

Isolation complete
dust free, soul pure, he feels great

132. HUMOR MILL

I'd rather not go to temples and churches

ah, the tiring processes of ceremony !

I can't stand the rigor mortis

the cumbersome sequence of formality

My humor mill comes to a screeching halt

by lack of lubricity

133. DETACHMENT

Flowers and mortals bloom and doom

impermanent is the world

Sending calves away cows moo

because of their lingering attachment

When I die like the falling leaf

I shall go free in detachment

134. SIMPLE LIFE

Seeking for wealth and power
megalomaniacs run for vanity

Conflicts confusion continue
the world is noisy, busy, gory

I shall lead a simple life
keeping my mind in sanity

135. ALL HAPPY

Frogs croak in pond

bees buzz probing deep into honey glands

Algae swim free in water

Azaleas smile in arid land

All happy

each taking own stand

136. ENJOY ALIVE

Motorists are out

for a fresh freeway drive

Inchworms total deaf, flies half-blind

still they live well and thrive

All born in odd shapes, sizes, skills

with own traits, talents, tastes, enjoy alive

137. ECHOES

Saints and villains
are obsessed with super egos

Mohammed, Jesus, Adolf, Joe
were such heroes

We seem only value
lasting legacies of positive echoes

138. PRECIOUS

Millions perish in wars
bodies pile dung-deep

In the eagle-eyed war mongers
they're only worms that creep

For the enlightened mind
every life is precious to keep

139. DIVERSITY

God's Laws dictate conformity

Prominent politicians play God's authority

They urge folks to ignore their diversity

140. PRAYER

Many attend churches and temples

feel relieved there

Prayers free us from confusion and conflicts

so people come from everywhere

Since the Lord is omnipresent

confession and supplication can be made anywhere

141. ENLIGHTENMENT

Because of greed, anger and stupidity

world conflicts never end

Greed unfulfilled, one gets angry

following anger, one acts stupid

Stupidity brings trouble

only by enlightenment can the world be on the mend

142. SILENT AFAR

Bees buzz, birds twitter, dogs bark
under our great star

People jabber as they walk and work
roses smile quiet, lips ajar

While the weak speak, the meek shriek
stars blink silently afar

143. STAND TALL

Losing power, pomp, pride
arrogant people pose chagrined

Scattering flowers, dropping fruits, shedding leaves
trees dance naked in autumn wind

Stripped off vanity
trees stand tall determined

144. VIGNETTE

Michelangelo's murals clutter with nude figures
lacking are the landscapes with mists and mystery

Peeling off the last veils of Mother Nature
we lose her divine beauty

Vignette is Muse's evening dress
our fantasy dallying with the Goddess of Liberty

145. ETERNITY

Light, air, water shimmer

ever flamboyant

Nature's charm endless

while fleeting life's fluent

I'd find moments of eternity

in my Shangri-La if impermanent

146. LIFE CANDLE

Things and events unfold only to fade away

all phenomena never eternal

Attachment brings disillusionment

life shifts as the day, diurnal and nocturnal

My life candle burning still

only ephemeral

147. LIFE EASY

Only grabbing never to release

filling never to empty

Ever drinking more thirsty

earning for more money

Only upon death

comes life easy

148. NATURAL

Come spring, flowers blossom

excite not, their death inevitable

Come autumn, leaves shed

grieve not, their departure irreversible

Birth and death only natural

yet, many feel irritable

149. FEEL FRESH

Winds cease blowing in the field

I no longer hear the whistle of the rye

Clouds float passing over the lake

I do not see the reflections sail by

Agonies now clear through my bosom

I feel fresh under the blue sky

150. APOCALYPSE

We work most effective
in broad daylight

In the night the moon and stars urge us
to reflect our actions taken in the light

Lord's apocalypse profound
alternating day and night

151. BEING ALONE

Regimentation solidifies scattered minds

it's outcome seldom fair

Wars, religious or secular, are instigated

by charismatic leaders with great fanfare

I would not attend mass rallies

alone I can open my heart free in prayer

152. PERSPIRATION & INSPIRATION

Through isolation and meditation

Zen monks are enlightened and wise

Practicing mercy and compassion

they encourage the downtrodden to rise

With perspiration and inspiration

they succeed in their enterprise

153. ROAD TO ENLIGHTENMENT

Bloody ordeal in a holy mission

might lead me to rose-scent Eden of Jehovah

Enlightening self in the morning glow

I 'd stroll into lotus-bright Nirvana of Buddah

In an ebony night of Hegira following holy words

I may duck the holy sword of Allah

154. MEDITATION

Closing eyes, sedating passions
I open my heart and mind

Dismiss goblins, gurus, gods
by whom many are in capture

Meditation opens up Nirvana
where I reside in rapture

155. ASCETICISM

Fanning avarice, anger, apathy

industrial world drives folks crazy

The force of human instincts

kicks up worldly anxiety

Buddha teaches asceticism

enlightening us to be free

156. EFFORTLESS

Think sans thinking, talk sans talking

Learn sans learning, do sans doing

Work effortless and decisive in acting

157. NOURISH SOUL

Avid readers are often bookish timid

molding characters in rigid frames

Thoughts shall be innovated daily

freeing selves from mundane games

Neglecting constant philosophical nourishment

souls might snuff out their flames

158. LIGHTHOUSE

Day in day out

churning ocean waves moan

Trees brave at the shore

their frames badly twisted wind-blown

Amid constant cries of sea gulls

a rusty lighthouse stands alone

159. POSSESSED & OBSESSED

Naked ones in the pool
never complain what they wear

Ordained monks in the temple
have no income tax to declare

Only the rich and famous
obsessed grumbling everywhere

160. DAYDREAMERS

Godhead omnipresent far and near

Many obey his rules willy-nilly often with fear

In the vale of tears, daydreamers continue to appear

161. ELUSIVE

The soul free of greed and vanity
flies like spring breeze with fragrance

Nets of mosquito, fish or police fail to catch it
passing through them with nonchalance

It sings along con moto *in the flower garden*
blooming in complaisance

162. AGE NOT

Knowledge is power, so said Bacon
yet, if overstocked, it turns life gray

Books often make us indecisive
no bold actions turn out to play

Mortals age but pure souls do not
transcending time and space all the way

163. SIMPLE & SERENE

Producing and consuming goods galore

modern folks strife

Under piles of human wastes

little room left for a pleasant life

Pure soul resides simple and serene

not in the trash piles where germs rife

164. MY SPIRIT

A starlet blinking faintly in the sky
a grain of sand resting on the seashore

My existence in the vast time and space
as insignificant as a tiny fungal spore

Yet, my spirit is as vast as the Cosmos
embracing oceans and galaxies and more

165. WORLDLY TAINTS

Zen masters whack the backs of slumberous rookies

waking them up in the light of saints

A lightning holler of a holy monk ushers one

into Nirvana with which one never acquaints

A dazzling world opens up

cleansing away worldly taints

166. SOUL TAINTED

Cranes flocked over the temple walls
to land on the pines Solko* painted

Scratched trees were redone by a painter;
cranes returned no more on trees repainted

Birds cared only for the original
not the pictures redrawn by any soul tainted

*famous painter lived and was active during the reign
of King Jinhung (540-576) in the Silla Empire of Korea

167. SOUL FREE

Dictators egoistic

determined to regiment the mass in their organization

Free individuals struggle to guard themselves

against the tyranny of dehumanization

Freedom of soul

the real source of civilization

168. PHOTONS & SOULS

Quarks steadily sinking toward the black hole

while photons travel the space free

Bosons catch leptons and quarks

yet the elusive photons flee

Our bodies are caught in the net of Karma

like the photons, souls fly carefree

169. INTUITION

Attaining truth through intuition
Zen rejects logical abstraction

Only setting the self blank before the Nature
can a pristine experience come in attraction

Enlightening the mind in a confused world
Zen is in constant action

170. NO INTERMEDIARY

Daily plight

haunts people eerie

Saints teach us with dogmas rather impractical

politicians with messages incendiary

Using intuition Zen attains truth

direct with no intermediary

171. DIZZY & EERIE

In size, shade and shape

all things vary

Modern world cluttered with goods

consumers get weary

My monotony of mind

feels dizzy and eerie

172. PLIGHT

Charcoal and ice no more resemble

than the races of black and white

Salt and sugar can't be mixed

Christians and Moslems fight

Only the color blind and the enlightened

overcome the plight

173. COLOR BARRIER

It's only skin-deep, fence high
many hard-pressed overcoming the barrier

Acquainting skills, making money
the colored busy fighting for the career

Only the enlightened few
transcend it all sans tear and fear

174. AWAKENING

Reeds stand only pensive

never mind the dashing arrow

Scholars often talkative

and we never respect a sparrow

Some read tons of books awakening no soul

their minds quite narrow

POEMS

V. NIRVANA & SALVATION

Being aware of the Cosmic Laws of impermanence, salvation of our soul to Nirvana can be achieved by a quiet resignation toward our destiny. Dignified and positive posture at the rendezvous with death is an inevitable road to mortals encompassing universal existence including the mankind, flora, fauna and even the stars of galaxies.

175. SENSE OF ACHIEVEMENT

Birds flap away for their roosts

as the sun sinks red

Along the path of green meadow

hoes on shoulders, farmers take homeward tread

Laying down the pen

I stretch back on my bed

176. ENJOY WATCHING

Picked flowers soon wilt in the vase

Married beauties fast fade losing grace

I shall enjoy watching them at their place

177. CATCH THE MOMENT

We live moment by moment
not with the one passed nor that to come

Reminiscences are only ghosts no longer exist
dreams only surreal never wholesome

Failing to catch the moment alive
life's dull and tiresome

178. WITH GUSTO

A moment fresh is here now
not was and never will be

My life is only a small speck in universe
It's still mine precious and free

At this moment of my life
I'd live with gusto and jubilee

179. IT 'S TODAY

I gather roses today

tomorrows uncertain, no yesterdays remain

Stop reminiscing the past and dreaming of the future

now I drink water fresh out of the fountain

It's today, it's here now

the moment is real and certain

180. SOJOURN

I don't recall a previous life, if any
a reincarnation is not my concern

Many crave for a longer life
less mindful of its worth

None can live forever
I shall enjoy a life of temporary sojourn

181. BLESSED

Animals big and small, flowers bright and dull

all thrive free with pride and dignity

Snails envy no elephants

champignons never shy of flowers in the vicinity

All things live well

blessed in divinity

182. FANTASY

Crystal twin lakes nestle on a mountain top

dazzling sunlight is in charge

Red roses open fragrant in breezy air

twin peaks shimmer in the water like mirage

Down the lush valley is my oasis

a fairy waits for me with her entourage

183. LIFE VOID

Printed poetry pretty

because of the blank spaces

Rooms restful

because of the empty places

Life lovely

when mind is void after rat races

184. TECHNOLOGY

Circling around the world

in a single day

Beating glory of the Roman Empire

all the way

Technology has brought bounty

it's here to stay

185. BEING ALONE

Naked I'm not ashamed

poor I'm still proud

Meditate I see the Lord

whom I don't see in the crowd

I love to be alone

crying and singing out loud

186. RENEWAL

Water flows checking all flaws

Flowers blossom with no pause

Life renews under Cosmic laws

187. PHANTOM

Yes, Hegel, what's real may be ideal

But what's ideal may not necessarily be real

It's phantom being surreal

188. DISCIPLINE

Mirror gathers dust
keep cleaning when we may

Over enlightened mind clouds haunt
only by discipline can we fan them away

For the Cosmic conscious
mind-cleansing continues everyday

189. PYGMIES

Surrounded by star dust

the great Parnassian poses at heavenly ease

His poetic imagery, cadence, metaphor

run free like spring breeze

Scribbling out raw emotions

many poets appear as pygmalionesque pygmies

190. WRITTEN PAINLESS

The sight of Niagara Falls heavenly

as they pour down effortless

Spiders weave nets in the morn sun

free, fine, flawless

Writing poems my brain racks and hand doodles

when will be the day I write them painless?

191. NIRVANIC RAPTURE

Speak, sleep, eat little

Zen masters' ascetic venture

Killing desires, devils, anxieties

they maintain mental serenity

Passing through tunnels of torture

they take cold showers of Nirvanic rapture

192. CLOSE IN VIEW

Saints and gurus are no guide for my soul

blinking stars, buzzing bees are

Tripitaka, Bible, or Koran enlightens me little

my intuition seldom travels so wide and far

Paradise is close in view

as my heart and mind open ajar

193. IT'S NIRVANA

Retirees free if blessed in vitality

Out of pressures, they relax in dignity

Free from fame, money, sex, it's Nirvana sans vanity

194. IMMORTAL

Should only the rich and mighty live forever

The grassroot mortals would resent ever

Thank God we all die; none immortal, never

195. RESIGNATION

All things born to bloom and doom

Cosmic laws of unity and finity

Resigned I'm pious and joyous

196. SCATTER QUIET

Mourning and groaning mortals die ill at ease

Tigers being shot in pain they wheeze

Roses scatter away quietly in the breeze

197. FREE FROM AGONY

Cutting off strings of attachment

like the dandelion plumes wish I fly far in the sky

No longer drawn into swamps of worldly plight

where vanity and greed multiply

Completely free form agony

I shall live in Nirvana high and dry

198. ONE WAY STREET

An eternal sleep, farewell, rest in peace
poetic rhetorics abound in death treat

Death is a natural traffic of the way
moving only unidirectional with no retreat

Rendezvous with death
is a one way street

199. REST IN PEACE

Cultural avalanches

keep pressing tired souls dreary

Sights and sounds boundless

making the sensory organs turn weary

I shall rest in peace

buried nameless in the prairie

200. ABSOLUTE REALITY

Gunslingers everywhere
goblins, jinxes await on our ways holding breath

I don't know where, when, or how
I shall meet with my death

Death is the universal law for mortals
an absolute reality, not a shibboleth

201. NOT FREE

Often tempted to kill myself yet I can't proceed

Have works to finish books to read

Till then I won't be freed

202. BETTER DIE

Desires haunt me

better die avoiding the Faustian dilemma

Labors pressure me

better die easing the Sisyphean Karma

Pains kill me

Better die freeing the Promethean trauma

203. IDEAL DEATH

Life and death are the two sides of a coin

death hits us when we least care

People dramatize the event

creating rituals of emotional fanfare

I wish to die painless

facing my death without scare

204. ODE TO DEATH

Completely freed from daily torture

Letting down the life-long adventure

Now comforted in the bosom of Mother Nature